D0786288

COLORADO WATERFALLS

Photography by John Fielder
With Selected Prose & Poetry

Colorado Littlebooks

Westcliffe Publishers, Inc., Englewood, Colorado

First frontispiece: Fravert Basin Falls, North Fork of the Crystal River, Maroon Bells-Snowmass Wilderness

Second frontispiece: Parry primrose along a tributary of Vallecito Creek, Weminuche Wilderness

Third frontispiece: Conejos Falls, Middle Fork of the Conejos River, South San Juan Wilderness

Opposite: The Middle Fork of Anthracite Creek, above Lost Lake, West Elk Mountains

International Standard Book Number: 1-56579-053-7
Library of Congress Catalog Number: 94-060028
Copyright John Fielder, 1994. All rights reserved.
Published by Westcliffe Publishers, Inc.
2650 South Zuni Street, Englewood, Colorado 80110
Publisher, John Fielder; Editor, Suzanne Venino; Designer, Leslie Gerarden
Printed in Hong Kong by Palace Press

PREFACE

Considering that snow melts at 14,000 feet in elevation and oceans lap shores at zero feet, it is not unreasonable to assume that creeks and rivers might take a tumble from place to place. Colorado's precipitous elevations produce thousands of waterfalls and cascades throughout the state.

Many of these make huge drops, such as Conejos Falls and North Clear Creek Falls, while others merely cascade down steep deposits of boulders. No matter how sharp the angle of descent, Colorado's pure waters make a beautiful sight. The volcanic peaks of the San Juan Mountains to the southwest contain the highest falls, plunging over the edges of eroded rock faces. Others, such as those in Rocky Mountain National Park, disappear over heavily glaciated cliffs of granite.

Many hiking trails follow creeks, and most creeks contain numerous cascades and falls that are often not marked on maps. Though it is rewarding to search out Colorado's better-known waterfalls, I prefer merely to explore the backcountry, discovering new ones along the way. The route is often strewn with Colorado's most beautiful wildflowers, for the moist soils beside cascades and waterfalls are fertile enough to support profusions of Parry primrose, marsh marigold, mountain bluebell, and other water-loving plants.

Notice the visual quality of waterfalls from one time of day to the next. In the morning and evening, the warm glow of the rising or setting sun bathes cascades in pinks, yellows, and oranges, turning pure white waters into fruit punch. Beneath afternoon clouds, without the glare created by harsh sunlight, you can see the subtle lines of individual water strands. In fact, these times of the day are best for taking photographs of waterfalls.

A shutter speed of 1/30th second or faster will tend to "freeze" the motion of the waterfall, allowing it to appear on film the way it does to the eye. Slower shutter speeds, 1/8th

North Clear Creek Falls, along State Highway 149, near Spring Creek Pass

second or longer, will create that surreal "cottony" effect so common in my images. A two-second exposure will make cascades and falls look like vanilla ice cream. But remember that you will probably need to use a polarizing filter to allow the camera to make such a long exposure. And don't forget to use a tripod, for not even a brain surgeon can hold a camera steady for that long!

No matter what the visual effect, all waterfalls are thought provoking. Who has not sat beside a cascade and let his or her mind drift off into a world less demanding? Some of my own most lucid moments occur while enjoying the cool mist at creek side. Throughout this book, you will experience not only the glory of Colorado in photographs, but the thoughtful insights of talented writers influenced by the majesty and power of the natural world.

I sincerely hope that these words and images will allow you to unload some of the burdens of daily life, at least for a few moments. May they kindle a renewed sense of purpose in your life as well as a greater appreciation for things natural and primal. And may you have the opportunity to visit such places as depicted in the pages of this book — and lose yourself for a while in Colorado's waterfalls.

— John Fielder
Englewood, Colorado

Other books by John Fielder:

Colorado Reflections Littlebook
Colorado Aspen Trees Littlebook
Colorado Lakes & Creeks Littlebook
Colorado Wildflowers Littlebook
A Colorado Autumn
To Walk in Wilderness
Colorado, Rivers of the Rockies
Along the Colorado Trail
Colorado, Lost Places and Forgotten Words
The Complete Guide to Colorado Wilderness Areas
Colorado BLM Wildlands: A Guide to Hiking &
    Floating Colorado's Canyon Country

Also look for John Fielder's Colorado wall and engagement calendars.

Below Lion Lake No. 2, Wild Basin, Rocky Mountain National Park

"I gave my heart to the mountains the minute
I stood beside this river with its spray in my face
and watched it thunder into foam…"
— Wallace Stegner, Sound of Mountain Water

Above Arrowhead Lake, Gorge Lakes,
Rocky Mountain National Park

"If you want
To live long,
Just work.
Look, running water
Never stagnates."

— Japanese Zen Folk Saying

Bear Creek, Pierre Lakes Basin,
Maroon Bells-Snowmass Wilderness

"…And many standing round a waterfall
See one rainbow each, yet not the same to all,
But each a hand's breadth further than the next.
The sun on falling waters writes the text…"
— Gerard Manley Hopkins, At a Welsh Waterfall

Along the La Plata River, the La Plata Mountains,
near Durango

Overleaf: Cascade Creek, San Juan National Forest

"What a joy it is, to feel the soft, springy earth under my feet…to follow grassy roads that lead to ferny brooks where I can bathe my fingers in a cataract of rippling notes…"
— Helen Keller, The Story of My Life

Willow Creek, Willow Lakes Basin,
Maroon Bells-Snowmass Wilderness

"Running water is one of the universal parables, appealing to something primitive and ineradicable in human nature. Day and night it preaches — sermons without words."

— Torrey Bradford, The Clerk of the Woods

Colorado Columbine beside Johnson Creek,
Weminuche Wilderness

"The thunder of the water-wall
Fills the chasm with its fall…
And I see the high-hung watery dome
Breaking in a feathery comb
Of foam…"

— Friedrich Adler, By the Waterfall

Ruby-Anthracite Creek, below Green Lake,
Gunnison National Forest

"No check, no stay, this streamlet fears:
How merrily it goes.
'Twill murmur on a thousand years
And flow as now it flows."

— William Wordsworth, The Fountain

Chaos Creek, below Lake Haiyaha,
Rocky Mountain National Park

"…far off I watch the waterfall plunge to the long river, flying waters descending straight…
till I think the Milky Way has tumbled from the ninth height of Heaven."

— Li Po, Viewing the Waterfall at Mount Lu

Middle Fork of the Conejos River, below Lake Ann,
South San Juan Wilderness

"Rain drifts forever in this place
Tossed from the long white lace
The Falls trail on the black rocks below…"

— Andrew Young, The Falls of Glomach

Needle Creek, below Twin Lakes,
Weminuche Wilderness

"I come from haunts of coot and hern,
I make a sudden sally,
And sparkle out among the fern,
To bicker down the valley."
— Alfred Lord Tennyson, The Brook

Geneva Creek, Maroon Bells-Snowmass Wilderness

"What is harder than rock, or softer than water?
Yet soft water hollows out hard rock. Persevere."

— Ovid, Ars Amatoria

The Roaring Fork of Cabin Creek, above Peacock Pool,
Rocky Mountain National Park

Overleaf: Along Geneva Creek, Maroon Bells-Snowmass Wilderness

"The cataract, whirling to the precipice,
Elbows down rocks and, shouldering, thunders through.
Roars, howls, and stifled murmurs never cease…"
— John Clare, The Cataract

The Roaring Fork of Cabin Creek, below Chasm Lake,
Rocky Mountain National Park

"…when I face upstream I scent the virgin breath of mountains, I feel a spray of mist on my cheeks and lips, I hear a ceaseless splash and susurrus, a sound of water not merely poured smoothly down air to fill a steady pool, but tumbling live about, over, under, around, between, through an intricate speckling of rock."

— Annie Dillard, Pilgrim at Tinker Creek

West Branch of the Laramie River, Rawah Wilderness

"The earth speaks in magic, the magic of rainbows and waterfalls…. It is the magic of interacting sunlight and air and water… creating a constantly shifting kaleidoscope of wondrous riches on our turning planet."

— Steve Van Matre, The Earth Speaks

Ruby-Anthracite Creek, below Lake Irwin,
Gunnison National Forest

"With what deep murmurs through time's silent stealth
Doth thy transparent, cool and watery wealth
Here flowing fall,
And chide, and call..."
— Henry Vaughan, The Waterfall

Icy Brook, above The Loch,
Rocky Mountain National Park

"I thought back on boyhood
And summer, on the rock-shelved falls…
Routing from ledge to ledge,
A tumult at sunrise…"
— Galway Kinnell, Leaping Falls

Cascade Creek, near the junction with the Colorado Trail,
San Juan National Forest

"The current that with gentle murmur glides,
Though know'st, being stopp'd, impatiently doth rage;
But when his fair course is not hindered,
He makes sweet music with the enamell'd stones…"
— William Shakespeare,
The Two Gentlemen of Verona

Cony Creek, Rocky Mountain National Park

"Still waters are the deepest,
but the shallowest brooks brawl the most."

— C. H. Spurgeon, John Ploughman

Autumn along Lake Creek, beside State Highway 82,
above Twin Lakes

"The waterfall sang in chorus, filling the old ice fountain with its solemn roar…fit voice for such a landscape."

— John Muir, The Mountains of California

Along the La Plata River, the La Plata Mountains, near Durango

Overleaf: Ouzel Creek, below Lark Pond, Rocky Mountain National Park

"Someone must be
unstringing them wildly —
white beads shower down
without pause…"

— Ariwara No Narihira,
On Nunobiki Waterfall

Parry primrose along a tributary of Vallecito Creek,
Weminuche Wilderness

"Standing up on lifted, folded rock
looking out and down —
The creek falls to a far valley…
This living flowing land
is all there is, forever…"
— Gary Snyder, By Frazier Creek Falls

High above Black Lake, Glacier Gorge,
Rocky Mountain National Park

"If the voice of the brook was not the first song
of celebration, it must have been at least
an obbligato for that event."

— Hal Borland, Sundial of the Seasons

Along Ouzel Creek, below Lark Pond,
Rocky Mountain National Park

"And so never ending, but always descending,
Sounds and motions forever and ever blending…"
— Robert Southey, The Cataract of Lodore

Needle Creek, below Twin Lakes,
Weminuche Wilderness

Overleaf: Texas Creek, Collegiate Peaks Wilderness